'Tony for stock'; 'Horse embrocation'; 'Benbow's dog mixture'; 'Bronko's cough paste'.

BOTTLES AND
BOTTLE COLLECTING

A. A. C. Hedges

Shire Publications Ltd

CONTENTS

Eleventh impression, 1989.

COVER: *Victorian bottles and jars.* BELOW: *Green wine, olive sauce, cobalt castor oil, navy magnesia, and pale blue unguent.*

Digging for bottles in Warwickshire.

INTRODUCTION

At Sothebys early in 1974 they sold a bottle — an empty one at that — for £470,000. It was no ordinary bottle but one decorated with a splendid dragon and emanating from the Ming dynasty. The average bottle collector is unlikely to come across another even faintly resembling it, but the sale has helped to focus attention on the charm and attraction of bottles. The Victorians packed everything from tea to hair restorer in glass containers and then discarded them. They threw them out with the rest of the household refuse and there they are, in rubbish dumps all over the country, waiting to be dug up. Each and every non-machine-made bottle with its tears, streaking, irregularity of shape and strange neck angle is a collector's item. The colours — amber, cobalt, ruby, white and green — add to their attraction. Stone bottles and jars, too, with their uneven glaze and exquisite transfer markings have a charm seldom to be found in modern pots. Some collectors even find ginger beers more attractive than glass bottles!

Today there is a resurgence of interest in antiques and there are more collectors than ever there were. A few, disenchanted with equity shares, find a haven for their capital in antiques but most collectors just like to have beautiful things around them. They collect prints, enamels, horse brasses, paper weights, wine labels or old masters with such avidity that demand outstrips supply. Prices for the finer pieces inevitably soar out of reach of the man in the street and he needs must rest content with the more ordinary specimens. Moreover the situation is unlikely to improve for there are few undiscovered caches of Lowestoft china or Georgian silver and supplies dry up as items find their way into firm hands. The horizon confronting the bottle collector is vastly different. People are only now becoming interested and there are more than enough bottles to go round. Some day, of course, even this seemingly inexhaustible supply will dry up and there are already signs that some bottles (those that once contained Warner's Cure-alls for instance) are more rare than was previously thought.

3

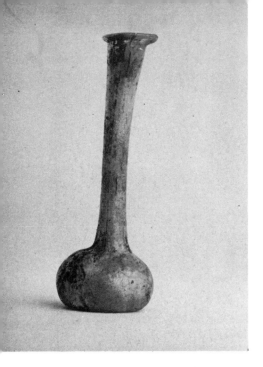

ABOVE LEFT: *Roman glass bottle dating from the first century A.D. and used for body oils and perfumes.* ABOVE RIGHT: *Seventeenth-century wine bottle with string ring.* BELOW LEFT: *Late seventeenth-century wine bottle.* BELOW RIGHT: *Squat wine bottles were common between 1710 and 1790.*

Pontil marks filed flat and the deep kick-up on a seventeenth-century wine bottle.

BLOWING A BOTTLE

The earliest containers were made from shells, gourds and animal skins and it was not until the beginning of the sixteenth century, when refugees from the Netherlands poured into the country, that a glass industry was established in England.

This was particularly odd because the art of making glass was known to the Egyptians and Syrians before 1500 B.C. Their technology too was sufficiently advanced for them to know how to colour it. Cobalt in the mix produced blue glass, iron oxide green; and appropriate measures of copper oxide added at different temperatures resulted in red, emerald, or even light blue.

The Romans in Britain used glass extensively for both household and decorative purposes but they imported it from the continent. The first English glass makers settled in the south, on the edges of the great forests, where wood, needed to supply both the potash used in the process and fuel for the furnaces, was plentiful. A mixture of sand, potash and lime was first heated in a clay crucible to a considerable temperature, and then, to speed up the process, small pieces of 'cullet' or broken glass were added. A chemical reaction then took place and the mixture transformed into molten glass. The glass maker allowed this to cool a little before scooping up a measure with his blow iron. Then by blowing down the tube he produced a bladder or 'gob' of glass. Sometimes he shaped it by rolling it gently over a flat stone or stretching it with specially constructed tools, but more often than not he achieved the desired shape by spinning the rod between his fingers or swinging it from side to side. The bottle was next allowed to cool until it was hard enough to be sheared off the end of the blow iron and then placed on a shelf in the furnace to anneal. The glass now had great strength and the first commercial bottles — those long narrow-necked vials much favoured by alchemists and apothecaries — were produced in this way.

These early bottles were crude by modern standards and their sheared lips made them unsatisfactory drinking vessels but by 1650 this snag had been overcome. Before the bottle was broken off the blow iron, another operative, usually an apprentice, put his solid iron pontil rod into the crucible and with the molten glass he extracted welded it to the bottom of the bottle. The master man then sheared off his blow iron leaving the bottle attached to the pontil rod. He then took it from the apprentice, thrust the irregular

neck into the furnace and, when the glass again became malleable, rolled the lip over a flat stone until all irregularities were removed. The bottle was then broken from the pontil rod and left to anneal as before.

It was now the base of the bottle that was uneven and this remained a great inconvenience until by accident an apprentice discovered the secret of the 'kick-up'. This indentation, still to be found in the bases of many wine bottles, was produced by pressure being applied to the pontil rod before the blow iron was sheared off. As a result the bottle had a more stable base and could be used as a decanter on the table.

Over the years manufacturing processes continually improved but the transition from the free-blown to the modern machine-made bottle was not achieved overnight — a study of the bottles themselves is proof of that.

BELOW LEFT: *Squat rolled-lip bottle.* BELOW RIGHT: *Free-blown bottle from the nineteenth-century also needing an osier base.*

WINE BOTTLES

Originally, wines were stored in the wood and carried away by customers in their own leather or stoneware jugs. Most of the stoneware, often inscribed with the mask of Cardinal Bellarmine, an Italian prelate bitterly opposed to the Reformation, was imported from the Netherlands. It was customary for the drinker to show his contempt for the Cardinal by quaffing the wine and then smashing the container. From the beginning of the seventeenth century, however, glass containers came into use. They were globular in shape, had no flat base, were pale green in colour and light in weight, and to enable them to stand erect on the table were usually encased in baskets made from osiers. Wanded bottles like these were blown until the middle of the eighteenth century — compelling most

BELOW LEFT: *The cylindrical bottle was introduced about 1800 to meet the vogue for binning.* BELOW RIGHT: *The seal on this bottle dating from about 1790 bears the initials of All Souls' Common Room.*

manufacturers to employ their own basket weavers — despite the introduction in 1650 of a dark green bottle with an onion shaped body and a long neck. This 'shaft and globe' bottle was easy to make and was manufactured until 1680 when its instability brought about the introduction of newer bottles with shorter necks and more cylindrical shoulders. Kick-ups too became wider and deeper.

These early bottles were sealed with wads of oiled hemp and later by loose fitting wedge-shaped corks tied down to a 'string ring', a ridged band on the neck just below the lip. In consequence bottles were stored the right way up, but as soon as the corkscrew was invented and it became possible to use tight-fitting corks, they were stored on their sides. The day of the onion-shaped bottle was over and squat wine bottles with necks as long as their bodies became the vogue, particularly for wines imported from France.

Soon these Burgundies and clarets, due to discriminatory tariffs, were ousted from popularity by port. This wine matures in the bottle if it is stored on its side, the cork kept moist and the bottle airtight. Even the squat bottle was not the most suitable receptacle for binning and gradually bottles became less dumpy and their sides more vertical so that by 1750 the cylindrical bottle had evolved.

SEALED BOTTLES

In the seventeenth and eighteenth centuries men of wealth considered it prestigious to collect wine in specially made bottles with their own seal embossed on the shoulder. This was usually the coat of arms, crest or name of the owner and in his diary for 1663 Samuel Pepys expresses his pleasure at his visit to 'Mr Rawlinson's where I saw my new bottles, made with my crest upon them, filled with wine'. When sales of wine in the bottle increased, clubs and taverns also had their own sealed bottles made and many have been found in Oxford. These old seals, unlike their modern counterparts, were produced by pressing a metal seal into a molten blob of glass applied to the completed bottle.

Armorial bearings are often a very good guide to the date of a bottle and towards the end of the eighteenth century sealed bottles were made bearing the initials and coats of arms of the colleges at Oxford and Cambridge. These bottles, however, were not the property of the college but of the wine merchant supplying the common room.

CASED GINS

Although in the eighteenth and early nineteenth centuries port was the favourite tipple of the well-to-do, the working classes overwhelmingly preferred gin. This was imported from Holland and, together with its cheap English imitation (often little better than hooch), was sold on draught, sometimes from barrels in the street.

Most of this 'Dutch courage' was imported in square bottles so designed that one dozen would fit conveniently into a wooden case. The bottles, mostly amber and brown, were blown in wooden moulds with slightly tapering sides which made easier the removal of the finished bottle. Some of the earliest bottles, before the technique was perfected, had sagging sides and were far from satisfactory. The short strong necks on these bottles were created by the blower pushing his iron inwards and producing a double thickness of glass at the neck before removing it from the body of the bottle. Even today bottles of this shape are favoured by some distillers.

ABOVE LEFT: *Stoneware container used for wine before the era of the glass bottle.*
ABOVE RIGHT: *A crested-seal bottle and a three-piece moulded bottle with applied lip and embossed 'Imperial Measure' on the shoulder. The embossed seal reads 'J. W. Watts, wine merchant, Coleford'.* BELOW LEFT: *A green Maraschino liqueur bottle, nearly eleven inches tall, with the original seal of Zara on its shoulder.* BELOW RIGHT: *Two embossed cased gins with differing necks.*

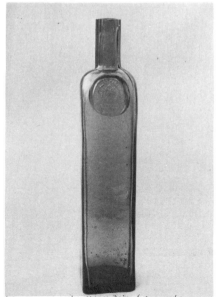

9

ABOVE LEFT: *Swing-stoppered bottles, the smaller embossed 'Please return this bottle value 2d'.* ABOVE RIGHT: *Cherry brandy, rare milk-glass cased gin, and bottle for bitters.* BELOW LEFT: *Giant Whitbread display bottle with quart beers alongside.* BELOW RIGHT: *Embossed beers with blob tops designed for internal screw stoppers from about 1890-1900.*

ABOVE LEFT: *Improved internal screw beer bottles heavily embossed date from about 1910.*
ABOVE RIGHT: *Straight-sided beer with crude string ring to take a hemp cork.*

BEERS

Originally beer, like wine, was drawn from the wood and carried away in stoneware or leather containers. The earliest beer bottles resembled those used for wine but as a great deal was brewed in the home and a heavy tax was levied on glass there was little to encourage the spread of bottled beers. Doctor Alexander Nowell had discovered by 1600 that secondary fermentation takes place in the bottle and if it were adequately sealed the quality of the beer improved, but in those days there were no adequate seals, only wired-on corks. Other closures, including metal clamps, were tried but it was not until the introduction of the internal screw stopper in 1872 by Henry Barrett that the problem of bottling beer was solved. The early bottles adapted for this new stopper had bulbous lips known as 'blob tops' but by the early years of the twentieth century techniques had improved so that no very pronounced expansion of the lip was necessary. Despite the invention of the swing stopper in 1875, the internal screw stopper was without serious rival until automatic machinery for filling and capping bottles was introduced. Then the crown cork patented in 1892 by an American, William Painter, superseded it.

ABOVE LEFT: *The unusual mineral on the left emanates from Buckley & Kelly of New Orleans; Lamont's Patent Bottle is in the centre, and a blob-top ginger beer on the right. The Lincolnshire cucumber in the foreground is unique to that part of the country.*
ABOVE RIGHT: *The original egg-shaped Hamilton bottle with blob-top introduced in 1814.*
BELOW LEFT: *A Codd-Hamilton hybrid in a metal stand alongside a square-shouldered Codd variety. The cap and plunger supplied with the mineral is also illustrated.*
BELOW RIGHT: *Green, aqua and amber-coloured Codd minerals.*

The flat-bottomed Hamilton not designed for internal screw stopper was made before 1872. The Codd to its right began to be superseded by the straight-sided screw-topped mineral about 1890. The embossed machine-made crown-top bottle dates from about 1910.

MINERAL WATERS

The art of manufacturing carbonised mineral waters was discovered in 1772 by Joseph Priestley and this new drink presented the bottle manufacturers with a major problem. The earlier producers of minerals, such as Joseph Schweppe, who started business in Bristol in 1794, used earthenware bottles but the gas permeated through the skin and the minerals became flat. In consequence mineral manufacturers switched to glass bottles similar to those used for wine, but the gas pressure inside built up to such an extent that there was a risk that the cork would blow out. This disaster could be prevented only if the bottles were stored on their sides so that the corks remained moist and tight in the neck. Most shopkeepers were reluctant to store bottles in this way but they had little option once the egg-shaped mineral-water bottle, introduced in 1814 by William Hamilton, came into general use about 1840. To overcome its disadvantages a flat-bottomed version was

ABOVE: *Rose's lime juice, Idris mineral and Valenio tonic wine.*

designed in 1870, but egg-shaped Hamiltons long continued in use. The cork stopper was retained by Schweppes until 1903 when the bottle was fitted with a crown cap. It remained in general use until the end of the First World War.

Throughout the second half of the nineteenth century thousands of closure patents were lodged with the authorities, for it was apparent that the wired-on cork had many disadvantages and prevented the proliferation of shapes in mineral bottles. The most ingenious and successful solution to the problem was that provided by Hiram Codd in 1875. His closure was effected by a glass marble being forced on to a rubber ring in the neck of the bottle by the gas generated by the carbonised drink. By means of a wooden cap and plunger supplied to every customer, the marble was forced down the bottle until it was trapped in two lugs constructed in the neck. The contents could then be poured out with ease. Codd himself took out over fifty additional patents in an attempt to improve his bottle, including one using an oval marble in an effort to make it less attractive to small boys. Breakages were enormous! Nevertheless, despite the introduction of the internal screw stopper in 1872, the Codd survived until about 1930 when it was superseded by the crown capped bottle.

RIGHT: *Internal screw-stoppered ginger beers.*

ABOVE LEFT: *Earthenware drug containers.* ABOVE RIGHT: *H. H. Warner started his patent medicine business in New York in 1879 and marketed his twenty 'cures' in these distinctive bottles heavily embossed with an old-fashioned safe.*

MEDICINES

From the earliest times man preserved his solid drugs in earthenware vases and his liquids in narrow-necked vials. Tapering bottles date from medieval times and from this shape the straight-sided cylindrical bottle gradually evolved. Medical inspection bottles, 'urynalls' as they were called, were being manufactured by John Le Alemayne as far back as 1597, and octagonal moulded vials were in use from approximately the same time. In those days barbers were the country's surgeons and they, like apothecaries, favoured square sectional case bottles and dark green globular bottles, which were still being manufactured in 1900. Patent medicines appeared towards the end of the eighteenth century and the manufacturer often marketed his product in odd-shaped, easily recognisable bottles. With the introduction of hinged moulds in the early nineteenth century chemists tended to emboss contents and dosages as well as their own names on the bottles. This craze for embossing was carried to extreme lengths in the latter half of the century by the manufacturers of quack cures, but the Victorian chemist preferred the acid-etched cylindrical bottle for his own stock. Medicine bottles are usually known as flats, rounds, panels, or ovals according to their shape.

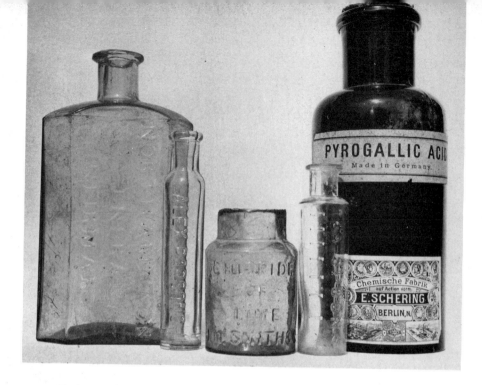

ABOVE: *Embossed and labelled medicines and chemicals.* BELOW: *Victorian poisons.* RIGHT: *Glass blower at work (photograph by courtesy of the Glass Manufacturer's Federation).*

ABOVE LEFT: *The schnapps bottle was in common use for many years before Jacob Schweppe used an earthenware bottle for his minerals.* ABOVE RIGHT: *Attractive transfer on rennet jar.* BELOW: *Manufacturers of ink, adhesive, Japan black and paste preferred earthenware containers.*

Stoneware gin and whisky containers.

STONEWARE

The most common containers in the seventeenth century were made from earthenware but its share of the market declined in the face of competition from glass. By 1850 most beers, wines and spirits, with the exception of gin, were available only in glass bottles, although earthenware retained its popularity for cider and vinegar. Fortunately the Victorian revolution in packaging provided new outlets, and preserves, ink and household necessities were marketed in earthenware containers of all shapes and sizes.

The ginger-beer makers remained loyal to the stone bottle, later adapted to take the internal screw stopper, until well into the twentieth century. They had used incised marks on their bottles for years but these were discreet and easily overlooked — no match for their competitors' lavishly embossed glass bottles and elaborately printed labels — and so from about 1890 they began to transfer-mark their ginger beers, though early specimens are rare.

ABOVE LEFT: *Incised stoneware beers.* ABOVE RIGHT: *Incised mineral, sealed and transfer-marked ginger beers. Those indicating that a refundable deposit was payable on the bottle are much sought after.* BELOW LEFT: *Stoneware remained popular for muff and foot warmers.* BELOW RIGHT: *Transfer-printed ginger beers.*

ABOVE: *Two-toned internal screw-stoppered ginger beers.*
BELOW: *Transfer-marked ginger beers designed for cork stoppers.*

ABOVE LEFT: *Embossed bottles for household products.* ABOVE RIGHT: *Embossed wines and spirits.* BELOW LEFT: *Embossed beers from Ind Coope, Adnams and Michie.* BELOW RIGHT: *Transfer-marked beer and an embossed beer with a printed label.*

22

EMBOSSING

Embossed bottles have a great appeal. They came into fashion with the general adoption of the hinged mould that permitted a plate carrying a message punched in relief to be placed in the mould. At first only the manufacturer's name and that of his product appeared on the bottle, but it was such a valuable medium for advertising that patent medicine manufacturers, growing fat on a gullible public, were soon ordering bottles in their thousands, all embossed and all claiming the most fantastic cures.

Most manufacturers followed this example and by 1895 about three-quarters of all the bottles made were embossed; but from the turn of the century, in the face of competition from the mass-produced machine-made bottle and the cheap printed label, embossing gradually declined.

MOULDS

Approximate dates can often be assigned to bottles from a study of their mould seams, but it should be remembered that the complete transition from one technique to another often occurred over many years. The earliest bottles were free-blown, but as their manufacture was time consuming and their uniformity of capacity could not be guaranteed, improved methods of production were needed as the demand for bottles increased.

Manufacturers, aware that moulds had been used by both the Egyptians and Romans, began to blow the bodies of the bottles in wooden moulds — usually square in section — hollowed out of solid pieces of timber, but try as they might, they were unable to form the shoulders, neck and lips in the mould. These were always applied by hand. The increased demand for cylindrical bottles was met by the invention of the hinged two-piece wooden mould which permitted the formation of the shoulders as well as the body of the bottle in the mould but the neck and lips were still applied by hand. Early nineteenth-century metal moulds made it possible for all but the lips to be formed in the mould. These bottles were often blown in three distinct moulds — the body in one, two identical shoulder and neck sections in the others. These were then brought together, more molten glass introduced, and the complete bottle produced minus only its lip. From about 1850 clamps were used to hold the bottle whilst the lip was applied and the pontil rod became obsolete.

Whisky flasks and other flat bottles were often made in strap moulds producing seams only along the edges and thus leaving the face of the bottle available for the embosser and acid etcher. Seams were also avoided by rotating molten glass in a mould previously coated with soap, beeswax and sawdust. The bottles so produced are regular in shape and there is little chance of them being mistaken for free - blown bottles with all their 'blemishes', faulty neck angles, pontil marks and kick-ups. Nowadays the making of bottles is a fully automated process, the first machine having been patented in 1887, and the mould seam runs through the lip as well as the body of the bottle.

ABOVE LEFT: *Early moulded sauce bottles with sagging sides.* ABOVE RIGHT: *Moulded wine with hand-applied neck and lip; three-piece moulded beer; hinged metal-moulded mineral.* BELOW LEFT: *Turned mould bottles with ground glass stoppers.* BELOW RIGHT: *Blob tops for cork, internal screw and an improved internal screw stopper.*

ABOVE: *Embossed whisky pumpkins and acid-etched coffin.*
BELOW: *Whisky coffins made in strap moulds.*

ABOVE LEFT: *Bottles with sheared, rolled and pouring lips.* ABOVE RIGHT: *Laid-on ring lip; applied lip on moulded bottle; collar below lip.* BELOW LEFT: *Various sauces including beehive pepper sauce.* BELOW RIGHT: *Glass-stoppered bottles.*

Victorian bottles with sheared lips and burst tops.

LIPS

A sheared top bottle has its top cut off clean with a pair of shears. But this took an extra operation and, when making cheap bottles, the blower allowed the glass at the top of a filled mould to form a bubble which burst, leaving a rough edge. It was a quicker process.

These methods remained in use until the introduction of automated machine-made bottles. It is the natural lip left when the blow iron is sheared from the bottle and is ideal for inks, polishes and varnishes because the jagged edges of the lip bite into the loose fitting cork and make a perfect seal. The lip of a bottle used for drinking was formed by reheating its neck and then rolling it on a flat surface. Flared lips, much favoured for medicines, were made in a similar way.

Later the irregularities of the sheared lips were concealed by a ring of glass which made a good base for a loose-fitting cork. It was much favoured for bottles containing drugs and is known as the 'laid-on' lip. The 'applied' lip, which was moulded on to the bottle after it had been formed in the mould, strengthened it and enabled it to take a tight-fitting cork. The introduction of the internal screw-thread stopper in 1872 inevitably led to beers too being manufactured with applied lips. They tend to have an irregular finish, as the molten glass runs down the outside of the neck rather as melted candle wax sometimes does, and can easily be differentiated from those on modern machine-made bottles.

ABOVE: *Cure-alls: hair restorer, consumption specific, lung treatment, Mrs Winslow's soothing syrup, swamp root kidney and bladder cure, gout cure.*
BELOW: *Metal-cased bottles.*

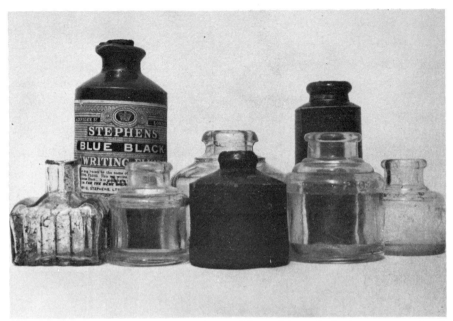

Inks in a variety of shapes and sizes, and second from right at the back a stoneware bottle for Reckitt's blueing, a dye used to whiten clothing in the wash.

HOW AND WHAT TO COLLECT

There are thousands of bottles as yet undiscovered in all parts of the country. The majority are buried in rubbish dumps and before long the avid collector, suitably garbed in old but warm clothes, stout boots and a serviceable pair of gloves will be seeking them out. If he is wise, he will have visited the public library and consulted large-scale maps of the district as it was in Victorian times and will have pinpointed the location of long-forgotten dumps. Some will have been built over but it is surprising how many remain untouched. Even the collector living in a town with every square yard built upon, has no need to despair, particularly if he keeps a watchful eye on the planning register. From this he may learn that a building erected on an old rubbish dump is to be demolished and another built in its

stead. Now he is on velvet — particularly if he can make friends with the site foreman! Sometimes an unsuspected dump is uncovered by reconstruction work and frequent visits to development areas will often reap dividends. It pays, too, to ponder over those old quarries, pits and disused mines shown on early maps but which have since disappeared. Perhaps too they have been filled with household rubbish. It was certainly normal practice so to do a century ago. Old people, particularly those living in the country, often recall the whereabouts of unrecorded dumps, for towns benefited from the organised collection of refuse for many years before the service was extended to rural areas. Cottagers, farmers and landowners all had to dispose of their own rubbish. A nearby hollow or

ABOVE: *Daffy's True Elixir and Crosse &
Blackwell's Eau de Rose — both
instantly recognisable by their shapes.*
BELOW: *Milk was sold from churns and
not bottled until the 1920s.*

pit, an adjacent coppice or even the village pond sufficed and a little detective work will often reveal the exact spot.

Most dumps, however, are unlikely to contain bottles manufactured before 1860, for until then, rubbish in most cities was taken to collection centres where scavengers sifted through it. Everything of commercial value was sold and the bottles ultimately found their way back to the brewers and bottle manufacturers. Fortunately for today's collectors, from the middle of the last century, rubbish was buried unsorted.

The majority of bottles will be those that were once familiar in every household in the land. Inks, both glass and earthenware, will be found in profusion — a constant reminder of pre-Biro and pre-typewriter days! The digger can be forgiven for thinking that the entire population once lived on pickles, preserves, sauces, ginger beer and light ale. Beer bottles in fact need not be very old to be collectable. So many small local breweries have merged with large national combines that their embossed bottles have become the stuff of social history.

Babies' feeding bottles turn up from time to time but less frequently than one would expect. This is perhaps due as much to the thin glass of the bottle as to the digger's failure to recognise an unfamiliar shape of feeder.

Many bottles, especially small unembossed ones which perhaps once contained perfumes, essences and powders, are difficult to identify unless they have a distinctive shape.

Veterinary bottles, too, are fairly plentiful and occasionally a glass-stoppered bottle will be discovered; but hip flasks and bottles in adjustable metal cases so beloved by the Victorian traveller have long found their way to the antique dealer.

Navigable rivers and streams can sometimes prove a veritable Eldorado, for in Victorian days large quantities of bottles were used as ballast and then thrown overboard. Before digging on land or under water, however, the first essential is to obtain permission.

Of course it is not essential to ferret around in rubbish dumps to be a bottle collector. Most diggers are only too pleased to dispose of duplicates and unwanted specimens, and many turn up in antique shops and on market stalls.

Cleaning and polishing

Before being washed, bottles recovered from dumps should be given 24 hours in which to acclimatise themselves to atmospheric conditions. They can then be dipped into a bucket of cold water and the surface dirt removed without fear of cracking the neck, invariably the weakest point of the bottle. Ingrained dirt and stubborn stains can be treated by filling the bottle to the brim and immersing it for 48 hours in a strong soda solution. Then it should be transferred for a day or two to a weaker solution of soda before being given a final rinse in clean water. Surface stains which do not respond to this treatment can be removed by gently rotating the bottle in a bucket of soft sand but the use of scouring pads should be avoided for fear of scratching the glass. Obstinate internal stains often vanish as if by magic if a little gravel in water is shaken vigorously in the bottle. Iron stains are particularly susceptible to this treatment if first softened with rust remover.

The cleaned bottle can be given a superb finish for all time if polished with cerium oxide, a difficult compound to purchase, but one sometimes available in lapidary shops. Failing this, an excellent result can be obtained by polishing with a light machine oil but the finish will not last for more than a few weeks.

Opinions vary as to the desirability of collecting damaged bottles. I see little objection in adding a damaged bottle but invariably it remains a reproach rather than a pleasure and I am always relieved to replace it with a better example. Bottles are beautiful things but there are so many of them that sooner or later limits have to be set on the extent of the collection. It is a decision however that should not be taken in a hurry and the collector should handle as many bottles as he can before deciding to specialise. Perhaps this book will help.

ABOVE: *Chemists' blue cylindricals, 16 inches and 12 inches respectively in height.* BELOW: *The old and the new from Apollinaris.*

ABOVE LEFT: *Defunct breweries: Crawshay & Young, Steward and Patteson, and Morgans.*
ABOVE RIGHT: *Hip flask and wicker-covered bottles.* BELOW LEFT: *Preserves and sweet jars.*
BELOW RIGHT: *Imperfect bottles.*